HOW TO MAKE

# BIG MONEY

IN YOUR OWN

# SMALL BUSINESS

HOW TO MAKE

# BIG MONEY

IN YOUR OWN

# SMALL BUSINESS

*Unexpected Rules Every
Small Business Owner
Needs to Know*

JEFFREY J. FOX

*New York*

Library of Congress Cataloging-in-Publication Data

Fox, Jeffrey J.
How to make big money in your own small business : unexpected rules every small business owner needs to know / by Jeffrey J. Fox.
p. cm.
ISBN 0-7868-6825-2
1. Small business—Management. 2. New business enterprises. I. Title.

HD62.7.F687 2004
658.02'2—dc22
2004040510

Hyperion books are available at special quantity discounts to use as premiums or for special programs, including corporate training. For details contact Michael Rentas, Manager, Inventory and Premium Sales, Hyperion, 77 West 66th Street, 11th floor, New York, New York 10023-6298, or call 212-456-0133.

FIRST EDITION

10   9   8   7   6   5   4

*This book is dedicated to the owners, officers and operators of Foxy Fast Lube, LLC.; Loondance, LLC.; Willimantic Car Wash Inc.; Foxy Franks, LLC.; Fox & Co. Inc. (and of other businesses bought and sold).*

# ACKNOWLEDGMENTS

Thanks to—

Michael Davitt Fox, BA, MA, LHD. Born 1885 in County Clare, Ireland. One of thirteen children raised in a two-room house in Miltown Malbay, then a tough town. Superintendent of Schools, Hartford, Connecticut. Staunch promoter of education, independent thinking, and entrepreneurship. Inspiration for Chapter VI. Died 1946.

Friends and clients, whose independent-minded input and editorial suggestions were gladly accepted.

Mary Ellen O'Neill, Executive Editor, Hyperion Books, who once again shepherded blank pages into a book, and Donna M. Ellis, Senior Production Editor, Hyperion Books.

Doris Michaels and Ben Salmon of the DSM Literary Agency (NYC), whose unrelenting enthusiasm and professionalism get the Fox book series published throughout the world.

# CONTENTS

HOW TO MAKE

# BIG MONEY

IN YOUR OWN

# SMALL BUSINESS

## Introduction:
## Why You Should Read This Book

*I*f you want your own small business, or if you own a small business, this book is for you.

Small business is where the money is. Five percent of American taxpayers pay 51 percent of the entire income taxes paid in the United States. That's very few folks paying very big money! Of that top 5 percent of big money taxpayers, 65 percent are small business owners. The average income of these small business owners is over $400,000. That's big money!

According to government statistics there are at least 25 million small businesses in the United States (a "small business" is one with fewer than 500 employees, and can be a corporation, a partnership, a proprietorship). Undoubtedly, there are, at any one time, millions more. For example, criminal enterprises don't usually register with the IRS. Waiters, taxicab drivers, lemonade stand operators, and paperboys (and paper girls) are small businesses. Caddies, babysitters, entertainers, and full-commissioned salespeople are small businesses.

Of the 25 million small businesses, about 20 million have fewer than 50 employees. Approximately 17 million small businesses have only one or two employees, including the owner.

Small business owners are known by many names: agents, entrepreneurs, capitalists, consultants, investors, inventors, franchisees, merchants, partners, promoters, operators, chiropractors, lawyers, artists, architects, bankers, carpenters, engineers, grocers, hairdressers, painters, plumbers, restaurateurs.

Successful small business owners come in all sizes, shapes, and colors; high school dropouts and Harvard MBAs; young and old; male and female; hardscrabble and to-the-manor-bred. They work hard. They create value. They generate lots of paychecks to pay lots of mortgages and tuitions. For better or for worse, they are in control of their destiny.

Small business is where the money is. It is also where

the brains are. Small business creates all of the net new jobs the U.S. economy generates each year. Small business generates fourteen times more patents per employee than the big fortune 1000 companies with massive research and development (R&D) budgets.

And small business is where the action is. The small business owner does more different things in a day than the CEO of a Fortune 500 company does in a month. Unlike top executives in big companies, the small business owner sells, buys, borrows, bills, collects, pays, invents, innovates, changes, guesses, decides, risks . . . and does so every single day.

The competent small business owner goes to bed every night worrying and thinking about meeting payroll, paying suppliers, paying back the banks, solving problems, bringing in more revenues, doing the right things, and doing the right things right. And every morning the small business owner gets up and finds a way to do what he or she has to do to make the enterprise succeed.

Big money. Small business. To paraphrase Calvin Coolidge . . . unashamedly, forthrightly, thank Godfully, "Big money, and small business, is the business of America."

# There Is a Lot New Under the Sun

*I*t is amazing how often one hears the old saying: "There is nothing new under the sun." It is doubly amazing how many people just nod in agreement at that stupid saying. "Nothing new under the sun" is an excuse for not thinking. The expression diminishes the innovation, the innovative, and the innovator. And the saying is dead wrong! Don't let that dismissive notion stall you.

There is a lot new under the sun, and truly new ideas hit the marketplace every day. It's a good thing Dr. Jonas Salk believed there was a new way to conquer disease and thereby invented the polio vaccine.

It's a wonderful thing that researchers are working on ways to beat other diseases, and to beat the resurgence of super-bacteria such as those that cause staph infections. Why didn't Thomas Jefferson and John Adams simply e-mail their brillant letters to each other? Or why didn't Tom pick up the phone and call John? Either approach would have saved weeks per letter. From whom did Stephen Stills steal his lyrics . . . Stephen Foster? And the next time you are mulling ticket options to fly from here to there, send a smoke signal to Icarus to see what he's offering. Maybe old Ic will fax you back some times and prices.

There is unlimited potential for innovation in new products, new ways of selling, new ways to serve the customer. Brewing and selling and serving coffee had been around for centuries until Starbucks revolutionized the business. Babies and toddlers were dropping baby bottles for generations until a mom invented the two-handled bottle. Auctions are as old as commerce, but eBay has built a huge business putting auctions online. (Oh, did Alexander Graham Bell also invent "online"?) And there must be a millionaire out there somewhere who put little wheels on suitcases. Each of these simple ideas was the foundation for an innovative business.

If you think you know a better way to give a customer what he wants or needs, you are probably correct. Brush off comments or "advice" such as "That's been done before," or "That's already been tried." Those thoughts are idea killers. Ignore the idea killers.

The people who care about new things and new ways and new ideas are the following—in order of importance—customers, owners, employees, suppliers, moneymen, taxers, community.

Ask the folks at the patent office if there is nothing new under the sun. The "nothing new" notion is patently absurd.

There is a lot new under the sun. Your idea could be a small business. Go for it! Bring it forth! It may provide your moment in the sun.

# One Difference Between Yes and No (or the Reason a Corporation's "Bad" Ideas Can Be Your New Business)

*O*ne difference between yes and no is what the words mean to the entrepreneur, the small business owner; and what they mean to the corporate executive, the corporate manager. To the entrepreneur the word *yes* means okay, validation, great, success, and go! To the corporate executive the word *no* means uh-oh, stay clear, problems, failure, and stop! The differing impact of these two little words on the small business owner and on the corporate executive is not glancing; it determines outcomes.

The corporate executive can hear the word *yes* ninety-nine times, and hear the word *no* but once, and not go ahead. The entrepreneur can hear the word *no* ninety-nine times, and the word *yes* but once, and go ahead.

Consequently, a great place for new business ideas is the corporation. Keep an eye out for the ideas corporate managers dismiss, ignore, throw out, refuse to consider. During the 1970s a leading U.S. importer and seller of beverages turned down the idea of importing bottled water. "Who would drink water from a bottle when they can drink it from the tap, and who would drink water with bubbles?" eloquently and rhetorically (to himself) bellowed the dope who knew there was no market for Perrier and Evian and Pellegrino. That millions of Europeans were drinking such products, or that millions of Americans had visited Europe, or had family roots in Europe, was proof enough for the entrepreneur who organized a small import business that became a big import business.

Paychex, the hugely successful business that provides payroll and other services to businesses with fewer than fifty employees, was launched after its founder, B. Thomas Golisano, pitched the idea to his bosses and was turned down. "We don't think it's a good idea" was the entirety of reflection that Golisano's top management gave his concept. Paychex is over a billion dollars in sales and growing.

Big corporations are chock-full of people who can't get past *no*. Big corporations talk innovation, but don't innovate. If you are working in a big company, keep your eyes and ears open. There are probably lots of untended ideas that would make a great small business.

# · III ·

## *Sources of New Business Ideas*

*H*ere is a grab bag of idea starters, of where to look, of routes to find opportunities for your own small business.

1. Look in the mirror. What do you do well? That skill could be the basis for a big money business.
2. Look within your family. Is there a family business you can take over? Or can you go to work for the family business, learn everything, and start your own?
3. Look in your present company. Can you

start a business doing something that your company is not doing? Is there a market your company should be serving, but is not?

4. Look at any ideas your company rejects or dismisses, or tries to do and fails. These are often small business opportunities.

5. Read magazines on franchises. Buy a franchise, or start a company in an industry that is growing rapidly, such as workout salons for women over thirty. There are numerous good franchise opportunities.

6. Provide ethnic products and services. Look at growing ethnic populations and sell to them what they want the way they want it. For example, what products do folks buy in the Dominican Republic that they can't get in the United States? Learn Spanish and sell to all Spanish-speaking customers.

7. Health-care services of all kinds are needed and growing as people age.

8. Watch the skills-oriented television channels, such as those that feature home repair, gardening, decorating. These shows represent trends and popular ideas. Is there a business organizing customers' garages? Is there a busi-

ness providing flower and shrub garden planting maps over the Internet? Is there a business managing the personal administrative affairs of busy people, where both spouses work, or travel extensively, or own multiple homes, or any combination of lifestyles that make organization a must?

9. Buy the company for which you work. Strategies to buy your company are called LBO, leveraged buyout, and MBO, management buyout.

10. Accountants, trust lawyers, corporate loan officers, business brokers, and the classified ads are sources of leads on companies for sale. Buy one.

11. Look at that business over there: Can you run one like it a bit better? That business you noticed on a recent trip: Is anyone doing the same thing where you live, and is there a need?

12. Follow through on one of your old ideas, one you've been telling people about for years. Follow through on your school project that outlined a new hypothetical business idea.

# The Small Business Owner's Success Blueprint

$T$o get started, and to be successful, you must . . .

1. Write a one-page crystal clear description of why your business will succeed. You must read this description to people aged fifteen to eighty-five, and if they get it, you've got it. (See Chapter XLIV for sample business description.)
2. Know that there are, or will be, customers for your business.

**3.** Calculate your breakevens. (See Chapters XLV and XLVI.)

**4.** Calculate the size of your market. (See Chapter XLVII.)

**5.** Know why you can sell the minimum number of needed customers; or why you can generate the minimum revenues needed to succeed.

**6.** Know how you are going to identify, attract, get, and keep customers.

**7.** Know how much money you will need to get started, or to keep going.

**8.** Know why a money source should make the money available to you.

**9.** Know your product or service's points-of-difference, and price that difference to its value to the customers (versus pricing to cover costs).

**10.** Know how you will provide or deliver the product or service.

**11.** Know what kind of people, if any, you will need, and have a plan to hire them.

**12.** Know where your business will be located.

13. Have a good name for your business.
14. Gird your loins, unsheathe your sword, and merrily sally forth into the marketplace.
15. And, most important, you are, or must be willing to become, your company's rain-maker. You must start selling and never stop!

# · V ·

## *Do What Comes Easy to You, but Is Hard for Others*

*I* f others are trying to do something, like building a solar-powered lawn mower, that is a clue that there is a market for someone able to build such a lawn mower. If there are lots of people trying to ride Brahma bulls, or going to law school, or writing software, then there is a market for bull riders and bull throwers. If you can do something with ease, that others find difficult, and there is a market for what you can do, do it. You will make money.

You will make money doing something that comes easy to you, but is hard for others to do, and for which there are customers. You will make money because you will give customers what they want and because you will have some kind of advantage over others trying to serve the market. Your advantage may be a gift for color sense, or an ability to deduce answers, or the skill to put people at ease, or having a prodigious memory. Whatever your advantage, it will result in a superior product or service; or a faster response to customers; or quicker entry into the market; or a lower cost basis; or any combination.

For example, if you can write compelling advertising copy, which is a rare talent, then you could start an advertising agency, or become a highly paid freelance copywriter. If you have an instinct for finding fish, you could become a for-hire fishing guide. If you have wonderful organizational skills, you could build a party planning business, or run philanthropic money-raising events (for which you are paid). If you have an aptitude for mathematics, you could start a jet airplane fractional ownership business, a gambling casino, or a tutoring business to teach kids algebra.

Don't diminish or dismiss a natural talent or skill. Too many people incorrectly believe that if they can do something with ease, then everyone can. Or because their talent comes easily, they diminish that talent as commonplace. When you diminish your talent as commonplace, (a) you won't work at your talent or genius to improve it; or (b) you won't value your talent for what customers will pay; or (c) you will do both.

To make money, you must work extremely hard on what comes easy to you. You must work, work, work; and practice, practice, practice to improve your innate talent. Just because a talent comes easy to you does not mean you are on easy street. Just because something valuable is easy for you does not mean you can take it easy.

The Hall of Fame baseball player Ted Williams, who was an absolutely awesome hitter, and who possessed phenomenal physical skills, was once asked how come hitting a baseball came so easily to him. "Simple," answered Ted Williams. "I take one thousand swings a day." Ted Williams went to batting practice, to the locker room, to his kitchen, to his bedroom swinging real and imaginary bats. He took 1,000 swings a day. Ted's 1,000 swings were probably 900 swings more than anyone else. And 1,000 swings a day is why hitting "came easy" to the great Ted Williams.

Doing what comes easy to you is only the starting point, but it is a starting point. Work at it. Practice it. Promote it. Value it. Sell it. Build a business around it.

# *It's Okay to Pick Fleas off a Dog*

*I*t is okay to own a company no matter what the company does, as long as the business is legal, ethical, and moral. It is okay to have a business in any industry. Don't snub any business. Don't look down on the business owner or the business that carts manure, or picks up dead carcasses from the highways, or rents rooms in flophouses to vagrants. Any business is okay if it is filling a customer need, operates within all laws, and won't earn you demerits from St. Peter (or from whoever greets you at the pearly gates of your higher power).

It is okay to pick fleas off a dog, especially if it's

your own dog. It is okay to pick fleas, or to sell fleas, if that is your own small business. It is okay to scrub toilets, clean dishes, wax boats, sling hash, muck out stables, milk camels. It is okay to do any job working for a customer, because all jobs can be done with dignity. You can own a small business making any product or providing any service. No matter how mundane your company; no matter how unglamorous; no matter how unfashionable, or how pedestrian and unsuitable for the social register crowd, ownership takes away any sting in doing your company's work.

So, pick those fleas. They're your fleas. It's your dog. It's your small business. Glory in it!

Are you feeling a little itchy?

## • VII •

### *First: Have a Customer*

*T*he most important factor to the success of your business (small or big) is to have a customer. Having a customer is more important than the business idea, the management, financing, plans, or anything else. This is rule number one and must never be forgotten or violated. Having a customer means that one person or many persons will absolutely buy your product now, or will buy it when the product is available.

Knowing you "have" a customer can come easily or, as is more often the case, can come with difficulty. The main character in the baseball movie *Field of Dreams,* when contemplating the building of a baseball field in the middle of an Iowa cornfield, neatly summed up the entrepreneur's dilemma: "If I build it, will they come?" You can determine if you have a customer by using market research, test marketing, instinct, or uncommon common sense. For instance, the drugmaker knows he has a customer for the cure for obesity. The toothpaste maker knows he has a customer for a toothpaste that actually whitens off-colored teeth. The lawyer knows she has a customer for the person who might gain financially from a contested will. The Internet auction house knows they have a customer because non-Internet auctions have flourished for centuries. The lady who starts a specialty cosmetics business, or an oatmeal cookie business, or a Christmas ornament business knows she has a customer because people bought her cookies and ornaments at a school fund-raiser, and then asked for more.

Having a customer is rule number one. Getting a customer is rule number two. Keeping a customer is rule number three.

## • VIII •
## *Small Business Owner's Business Priorities*

*I*n order of importance, this is how the small business owner must prioritize and allocate his or her time:

- Keep a burning focus on marketing and selling.
- Keep existing business.
- Grow existing business.
- Get new business.
- Do pricing, billing, collections.
- Have cash.
- Meet payroll.

- Have excellent people.
- Listen carefully to everyone.
- Train people.
- Have excellent product quality, as defined by the customer.
- Know how your product or service is different from what is offered by competition.
- Set goals.
- Delegate tasks down, down, down to the lowest level person competent enough to handle the task.
- Coddle suppliers.
- Coddle lenders.
- Review expenditures over $1,000.
- Complete the absolutely necessary administrative tasks that if not done now become a big problem later.

# The Small Business Owner, aka "The Rainmaker"

Your business exists for only three reasons: to solve a customer's problem, or to make a customer feel good, or both. There are no other reasons for your company to exist. It is every single employee's job, in any company, to directly or indirectly get and keep customers. So, if you are the only employee in your company, as is often the case, your job is to sell your company's products or services . . . to solve the customer's problem or to make the customer feel good. You are responsible for generating 100 percent of your company's revenues. You are your company's rainmaker!

A rainmaker is like the American Indian medicine man, who did his mojo and brought forth the rains that brought forth the crops so the people would flourish. The rainmaker brings in new customers, brings in revenue from new and existing customers, and keeps the profitable customers from going elsewhere. You, the rainmaker, bring forth the customer money that makes your company flourish.

If you are a one-person company, you must spend at least 60 percent of your time getting and keeping customers. Companies do what the boss does. So, if you are the CEO of a 10-person company or a 100-person company you must spend 60 percent of your time getting and keeping customers. You must do this so everyone else will do it. You must do this continuously, regularly, vigorously.

You are the rainmaker. Make it rain. Keep making it rain. Ring the cash register. Ka ching! Ka ching! You are the rainmaker!

# • X •
## *Selling Is Job 1*

*F*ord Motor Car Co.'s slogan "Quality is Job 1" is wrong: selling is Job 1. This is a critically important understanding for the small business owner. You must sell, or get people who sell, or both. Without sales revenues, you have nothing. For most small businesses, selling means reaching out to prospective customers, visiting the customers, asking questions, showing benefits, and asking for the order. This is true even for those small businesses that conduct business on premise, as in a store, restaurant, dealership, or doctor's office. It is not good enough to sit behind a desk, or stand behind a counter, and wait for customers to stream into your place of business. You must reach out to attract customers: advertise, communicate, promote, put up signs, get on the phone. The small business owner must make rain. He or she must sell to ring the company's cash register.

Many businesses quite correctly use advertising, yellow pages, promotions, signage, good location, and clever company names to attract customers. But don't just depend on advertising or publicity, for example, to do all the selling. Don't depend on a colorful brochure to do your selling: Brochures, and other marketing executions, can be a crutch. Every small business owner must always be selling      discreetly, proactively, obviously, continuously, politely, relentlessly, persistently, happily. There is nothing wrong with the dress shop owner, or cake baker, or candy maker, or lube shop owner, or dentist, or architect, or songwriter, or landscaper telling everyone they meet about their business. It is absolutely correct and proper for the accountant or limousine owner or computer trainer to give his business card to everyone.

If your customers do not come to your premises to buy, then you must go to them. You must constantly be getting leads, referrals, introductions, appointments. You must constantly talk to and call upon customers.

You must constantly present proposals, write specs for contracts, bid on those contracts. You must constantly throw your hat in the ring.

Quality is not Job 1. Quality is defined by the customer, not the seller, and is expected by the customer to be as advertised or claimed. Acceptable quality, to the customer, is required just to play the game. Acceptable quality and products priced to value are minimum requirements to be in business. Acceptable quality is so expected by the customer that verbose claims about quality are ignored.

Selling is Job 1, and if no one is selling, the business is dying. So, don't get discouraged. Don't worry about rejection. Don't be weary. Pick up the phone and call. Your customers and prospects want you to call. Call someone now! Meet someone now! Go talk to a customer now!

## · XI ·

## *Hire a Salesperson First*

The small business owner must be a salesperson. The owner might not be a great salesperson, but it is his or her job to ring the cash register. And you ring the cash register via happy customers. If you are not good at selling, hire someone who is.

Hire a salesperson to sell the product before you hire someone to make the product. Hire a salesperson to sell the house before you've built the house. Be sure there's a little, if not a lot of, salesmanship in everyone you hire. Everyone's job is, directly or indirectly, about getting (or selling) and keeping (or reselling) revenue-paying customers.

Only hire salespeople who can sell.

Only hire salespeople who are motivated, happy, hardworking, healthy, hungry, courteous, fearless, organized, persistent, polite, relentless, open-minded, well-mannered.

Once you've hired a salesperson who sells, don't abdicate all the selling to him or her. Keep talking and listening to customers, and give the customers what they will pay for. That's selling. Keep selling.

After you hire one salesperson who can sell, hire another.

# *Hire Ex-Paperboys*

The kid, boy or girl, who gets up at 5:00 A.M. every day, regardless of the weather, and regardless of summer vacation, to deliver newspapers in the dark, has got the goods. The successful "paperboy" is dependable and a self-starter (even if Mom has to occasionally play backup to the alarm clock). The paperboy is physically strong: It is not easy to lug a load of papers, especially the Sunday monsters, and get them to the customers before breakfast. The paperboy is independent, mentally tough, and not influenced by peer pressure: It is socially difficult to be a paperboy when all of one's peers are driving SUVs and taking tennis lessons.

The paperboy learns the rules of doing business. He, or she, is compensated based solely on performance; there is no guaranteed salary. The more papers he sells and the more customers he gets and keeps, the more money he makes. Good performance also generates gratuities. The paperboy has to collect money, order the correct number of papers, balance inventory, keep records, make payments. The paperboy organizes helpers. If the paperboy can't deliver, due to illness or a family event, he or she must have trained, at-the-ready substitute carriers. The customer must get the newspaper, and it is the paperboy's job to make sure that happens.

The successful paperboy, someone who has done the job for more than a year, is a hard worker, and a worker who gets things done alone. This is the kind of person you need in your business. You need people who value the job, and do the job well.

A PhD—paper hauler degree—from the schools of the streets is a better success predictor than a PhD from the schools of the ivies. Be more impressed with the person and performance than with prestige schools and pretty degrees.

Boys and girls who worked as paperboys have an edge. So, too, do boys and girls who have worked as caddies, cow milkers, lawn mowers, snow shovelers, babysitters, food servers, crop pickers, dishwashers, grocery baggers. Good child labor produces good adult employees.

And if you interview someone who washed out as a paperboy, wash your hands of that job candidate.

## • XIII •
# Hire Family . . . Until the Gene Pool Runs Out

*T*here are horror stories of family feuds in family businesses. The "shirtsleeves to shirtsleeves" description of the decline or death of a business is too oft too true. "Shirtsleeves to shirtsleeves" is a chronology: a grandparent or grandparents start a company with nothing. They work in blue-collared shirts. The second generation builds the business, creating a successful moneymaking enterprise. Everyone can afford a suit and dress shirt. The third generation, without the work ethic of its elders, or without the brains, or skills, or temperament, runs the business into the ground. Everyone is back in shirtsleeves. "Shirtsleeves to shirtsleeves" is a phenomenon often linked to a diminished family gene pool.

But there are millions of small businesses that flourish because the business is run by, or populated with, working family members. Good businesses are handed down from one good generation to the next. Family members can be employees or owners or both.

Hire the good workers in the family. You know them. You may have trained them, will train them, or observed their training. You know their strengths, which is where you put them to work. You know their weaknesses, which is where you don't put them.

You can trust family members. You will have similar, if not equal, goals. (The primary goal is to successfully stay in business so that all workers and owners benefit.) Family members are loyal. They will keep confidential matters confidential. Good family members won't steal. It is common that family peer pressure encourages good work habits.

Not everyone in the family is suited to work in the family business. Some people for legitimate reasons would rather not work in the family business, and do something else. Some people don't inherit the "work hard, work smart" gene. (This gene is located in the perspiration gland.) Some people don't inherit the "get along with others" gene. (This gene is located in the personal chemistry gland.) Some people are dumb. For these people, the gene pool has run out. These family members, if they need encouragement and support to prosper elsewhere, should be encouraged and supported to take a different path. You should hire everyone carefully and slowly. This is especially important when hiring family members. If a family member does not work out, the family dynamic is at risk. Failure in a family business can be fatal to traditional family interrelationships.

Hire family, but hire only those members who are genetically wired to work right.

# • XIV •

## Pay Steak and Eat Hot Dogs

*I*f you need a good person, or people, to succeed, then hire the best people. If you need people with special skills, or people with experience, or people who can do what you can't, then hire them. Pay as much to get the best person, or people, as you can afford. Pay them with money, with freedom, with courtesy, with a chance for some ownership, with thank-yous. Pay them more than you pay yourself if you must. Pay star employees steak. Pay yourself hot dogs.

Sacrifice the shrimp . . . and scrimp to succeed.

Invest in your future. Invest in building your business. Live on hot-dog pay until your business flourishes. Then add a little mustard. Perchance a glass of Dom Pérignon. Pay steak; eat hot dogs; and you will relish the result.

## · XV ·

## *Have a Penny Saver*

**B**en Franklin said, "A penny saved is a penny earned." In Ben's day, a penny was a pretty penny, but his advice is still relevant. If your business spends less than its revenues, you will make money. That's one of the secrets: bring in more money than goes out.

Large expenses, and once-in-a-while expenses, are always evaluated carefully. Various suppliers are reviewed. Bids examined. Prices compared. Prices negotiated. This is good business practice. But over time other costs of doing business get embedded in the business and are rarely reexamined, even over long periods of time. Because the pressure to bring in revenues is the highest priority, there is little time to review ongoing mundane expenses, such as add-on charges by the phone company. But add-on charges there will be, and surprise, surprise, the different bills for different cell phones will have different fees for unused features, minutes never used, and a gaggle of other "costs." The small business needs someone to look at all categories of expense, all bills, all suppliers, and to look for places to save.

The small business must have a penny saver. You must have a penny saver, not a penny-pincher. A penny saver gets the same services for less money without sacrificing quality. A penny saver discovers and eliminates misbilling, double billing, highest rates. A penny saver ensures that the company is getting the best price, the best rate that it deserves.

The penny-pincher underspends on customers, runs out of beer at the company picnic, and cuts costs that hurt the getting and keeping of customers. The penny-pincher "saves" money by reducing the number of shrimp in a shrimp cocktail, and thereby reduces the value the customer receives. The penny-pincher turns off the store air-conditioning at a certain date or time regardless of how hot and uncomfortable the store is for customers. The penny-pincher cuts muscle.

Penny savers regularly compare phone company long-distance rates, phone service fees, subscription prices, postage usage, insurance plans, credit card fees, interest rates, bank fees, suppliers' bills. This is not easy as the prices for many services are constantly changing, difficult to compare, and presented in a bewildering snowstorm of offers and deals.

The penny saver doesn't target those proven suppliers who personally service the small business. Long-term, dependable, trained suppliers help companies succeed and prosper. Switching long-term suppliers simply to obtain a lower price is dangerous. Lowest price is not always, if ever, the lowest total cost. (It may happen that long-term suppliers, for various reasons, are no longer able to deliver value, and must be changed . . . but go slowly.) The penny saver targets the impersonal supplier such as gasoline companies, utilities, trash haulers, and express mail companies.

The penny saver is not a scrounger. The penny saver is not cheap. The penny saver does not constantly drum beat and batter the company's suppliers for lower prices. However, the penny saver takes advantage of the fact that most salespeople don't sell on value, but on price. Consequently, the penny saver knows that most salespeople will immediately lower their price if asked this simple question: "Can you do any better?" The penny saver calls the credit card companies and asks for annual fees and late charges to be dropped, and often the charges are dropped.

Reward the penny saver based on costs taken out of the business.

Having a penny saver makes everyone alert to do the same.

When everyone sells, and everyone saves, the company succeeds.

## · XVI ·
## Pick Up Paper Clips . . .
## but Overspend on Customers

*P*aper clips cost money. Picking up a paper clip is picking up money. Throwing away a paper clip is throwing away money. Be prudent and frugal and turn off the heat, the air-conditioning, the water, the lights, the copier, the printer, and the coffeepot. There are lots of places to save money, but cutting money dedicated to getting and keeping customers is not one of them. Almost always, even in a tough economy, it is better to maintain or increase investment aimed at getting and keeping customers than to reduce it. Successful small business owners never let up on selling the customer, whereas it is common for large corporations, especially publicly listed corporations, to cut marketing and selling budgets.

A small public relations firm was working for a huge corporation on a number of projects. Two business events were unfolding at the same time: (1) The PR firm got a last-minute Friday morning call from its client's CEO, who needed help to write a speech he was to give Saturday evening, and (2) one of the huge corporation's customers was frantically trying to arrange a weekend delivery of badly needed product. The CEO was traveling Friday, but was expecting to spend some time in his office Saturday morning, some time at his home in the afternoon, and the evening at a hotel 1,000 miles away. The huge corporation was in a brutal cost-cutting mode, had cut back on customer service employees, and nitpicked every expense.

The public relations firm had three employees. The firm's owner assigned the speech-writing project to herself and to her two other employees, and all three did nothing else for five hours. The firm's owner did not see the last-minute request by her client as an irritation, but rather as an opportunity to make both her customer and herself look good. The firm's owner invested her company's total assets into the speech, even though she suspected she would probably not be able to fully bill, or get paid, for the time and value. Not knowing exactly when and where the CEO would be Saturday, the PR firm overnight expressed copies of the speech to the CEO's office, home, and hotel.

Late Friday afternoon the huge corporation's customer finally got through to a customer service rep. The customer service rep took the customer's order. The huge corporation's pricing policy was to ship two-day overland and charge its customers only for the cost of overland freight. The customer service rep knew the urgent need of the customer, but did not have the authority to arrange for the more expensive overnight delivery. The customer service rep's boss refused to authorize the extra expense for next-day shipping, saying, "Why did they call at the last minute? The customer should do better forecasting. It's not our fault they don't have enough product. We won't be able to bill for the extra charges. And, besides, our shipping budgets have been cut to zero."

The huge corporation's CEO received his last-minute requested speech on Saturday, and was delighted with how it was written. The CEO's corporation's customer received their delivery on Tuesday, but had to interrupt manufacturing for two days, costing them thousands of dollars in lost production. The

PR firm's invoice for the speech was grudgingly accepted by the huge corporation's VP of public affairs, but two of the overnight express charges were rejected . . . because the CEO did not sign for the two packages sent to the office and to the CEO's home!

The small public relations firm became a favorite of the CEO, and received several additional profitable projects. The huge corporation's customer found another supplier.

Overspend on the customer. If you do what's right, the customer will thank you with more business. If you cut an expense at the expense of the customer, you risk losing the customer. Instead of getting paid, you will get a payback. And payback, as in customer revenge, is tough.

# XVII

# Illigitimi non carborundum:
## Latin Is Definitely Not a Dead Language

*E* very small business owner should know some Latin. Whatever your educational background; whatever your ethnicity; whatever your native language, you should know some Latin. For example, every great salesperson, every rainmaker, embraces the meaning of "quid pro quo." Quid pro quo means "something for something." Quid pro quo means give something, get something. Give and get. The small business owner is always willing to give a sample to get a sale; to give a smile to get a happy customer; to give a good turn to get something in return.

"Carpe diem" (car-pay dee-um) is a terrific uplifting

commandment for the small business owner. Carpe diem means "seize the day!" Carpe diem exhorts the small business owner to make the best of today, the present. You can't change yesterday. You have today and tomorrow to improve your business. Do something! Carpe diem alerts you to "seize the opportunity." If you recognize an opportunity, something that could help your business, seize it. Research the opportunity. Think about it. Talk about it. If it's real, then carpe diem. Carpe diem is also a life rule: Cherish today. Find something good in today, no matter how bad it seems. Live big today.

And, of course, for certain, without doubt, you have the small business owner's back-to-the-wall, never quit, keep going essential Latin phrase: "Illigitimi non carborundum." A literal translation is "don't let the illegitimates wear you down." The saltier translation is stern advice to the small business owner: "Don't let the bastards get you down." You have to be tough, gritty, persevering to make your business successful. You can't let troubles, setbacks, dark times, dunning creditors, bad luck, bad weather, bad news, or customer rejection get you down. You must not let the illigitimi, regardless of their disguise, get you down. The illigitimi will hint that your idea will fail. They may suggest you don't have the experience. They will warn you about the risk, and all the money involved. The illigitimi would have you wonder that you are too young, too old, too brash, too sweet, too good. They will roll their eyes and smile ruefully at your enthusiasm. The illigitimi are dreary and deflating. The illigitimi are losers.

Ergo, "illigitimi non carborundum."

Live the motto of Avon Old Farms, a prep school for boys located in Avon, Connecticut: "Aspirando et perseverando." Aspire and persevere.

# XVIII

# *Practice the 60-30-10 Rules*

S mall business owners should invest their working time in 60 percent, 30 percent, 10 percent blocks. Here are four important 60-30-10 allocations.

    **1.** *Running the business.* Spend 60 percent of your time marketing and selling; 30 percent on making or providing product and service; 10 percent on managing and administration. So, market, make, manage . . . in that priority!

    **2.** *Selling.* Spend 60 percent of your selling time keeping and growing current customers;

30 percent on getting high-potential customers in the short term; and 10 percent getting high-potential customers in the long term. So, if you are spending 60 percent of your overall time marketing and selling, and 60 percent of your selling time keeping and growing current customers, you will spend 36 percent of your time (60 percent times 60 percent) meeting, e-mailing, writing, and talking to your cash register—ringing customers. In a sixty-hour small business owner minimum workweek, 36 percent means you are focused on current customers for 22 hours.

**3.** *Training.* Spend 60 percent of your training time enhancing your strengths, or your company's strengths; 30 percent of your time learning new concepts; and 10 percent fixing weaknesses. For those days when you are with another employee(s) you should spend fifteen minutes of that day training or teaching. If you are the only employee, spend fifteen minutes every day improving yourself. Fifteen minutes every "day" is about 400 hours in a typical year. If you spend 60 percent of that time, or 240 hours, honing strengths, adding

to strengths, sharpening your edge in the
market, you will realize a high return on that
training investment.

**4.** *Growing your people.* Spend 60 percent of
your people time with your superstars; 30
percent on high-potential people; and 10 percent on low performers. Don't be democratic
and invest your time equally. Spend your time
on winners.

Invest your time as you would invest money. The
first rule of investing is "don't lose." Thus, you invest
your time in keeping customers to not lose them. If
you had a choice, you would invest money in a good
performance company, versus knowingly investing in a
poor performance company. So too invest your time in
superstars and high-potential people. Invest your time
on strengths. Invest on improving.

The 60-30-10 rule is a powerful human asset allo-
cation system. Use it.

# · XIX ·

## Fame or Fortune? Pick Fortune

Don't seek fame. Seek fortune. Money over medals. Profits over plaques. Moolah over monuments. Rewards over awards. Cash over cachet.

If you are your company's product or you are 100 percent responsible for producing the product—as is the case for an artist, a one-person law firm, an architect—then fame (lots of publicity) can be an effective marketing tool. If you are not your company's product, do not seek fame. Rather, seek fame for your company, and for your company's products or services. Don't get your picture on the cover of *Rolling Stone* or *Time* magazine; get your product's picture on the cover. Your fame doesn't ring the cash register. It is your product's fame, and subsequent product sales, that ring the cash register.

Don't waste your time or money on anything that doesn't get and keep customers. Unless fame is part of your marketing plan, then fame is for ego. You can't put ego in the bank.

Work hard, sell hard to get your product famous. Get fame for your product and fortune will follow. After you get fortune, fame may follow . . . if you want it.

## • XX •
## *No Home Office!*

**U**nless you are single and living alone, a home office is not efficient. Even if you are single, your home office is in competition with your television, your refrigerator, your window views, your pets. If you do not live alone, but everyone is gone during the day, it still takes rock-solid discipline to not get distracted, to not answer the home phone, to not answer the doorbell, to not open the home mail, to not walk your pet ferret.

If you have a home office and your spouse or children or others are at home during the day, your day is dead. You can soundproof your "office"; you can padlock the door; you can chain a raging Rhodesian Ridge-back to the stairwell, and someone, somehow, will bother you. There are always a million errands, a million chores, a million questions to answer. A three-year-old is not being rude when she asks you to sew her ripped teddy bear: She has her priorities and they overrule yours. You are available, and someone will avail.

You can't bring customers to your home office. You can't do face-to-face interviews in your home office. You can't meet suppliers or people from other companies in your home office. You have to meet somewhere else, and that costs money and time.

As soon as you can afford an office outside your home, get one. Going to the office means setting the alarm, exercising, getting dressed for work, and going to work. It is a discipline. It is the opposite of rolling out of bed and sitting in front of your computer in your pajamas. (Lackadaisical work habits beget lackadaisical work.) An outside office need not be sumptuous. Barren and drab is fine. The iconic start-up garage is fine. A once-elegant old dilapidated building in the bad part of downtown is fine.

An outside office frees up room in your house or apartment. This is especially important for someone with young children, or with a small home, or both. More space means less stress, and less stress means a more productive life.

The home office comes with two deductions. There are tax deductions (you are allowed in the United States to deduct certain home expenses on your tax return), and there are deductions in your time, focus, concentration. The tax deductions never equal the cost of reduced productivity and reduced flexibility inherent with a home office.

# · XXI ·
## *Always Price to Value*

Whatever your product or service, you must decide how to price it, how much to charge. A veritable library of books has been written on the subject. Before reading those books, and before pricing your offering based on traditional methods, heed these three simple words: *Price to value!*

There are many ways to set prices. You can price your product or service by adding a markup to the production cost of the product. You can set a target gross margin at say 40 percent, and price accordingly. You can monitor competitors and meet, beat, or exceed their prices. Missing from all these approaches is a fundamental understanding of what your product is really worth to the customer.

Pricing to value means you set your prices as a reflection of the value your product or service creates for your customers. To do this, you must first understand what that value is and what it is worth to your customers.

When pricing a service, this means avoiding the trap of charging by the hour. Instead, consider the outcome of your service and what that might be worth to your customer, and set your price as a percentage of that outcome's worth.

For example, the typical private detective charges an hourly rate of say $150 per hour. If this detective agency gets an engagement to locate a missing person, or to do a background investigation on the management team of a company for sale, it does the job, multiplies the number of work hours times $150, adds in expenses, and sends a bill.

Another detective agency sets its fees differently. This agency sets its prices to value. When the owner of this detective agency is discussing the assignment with a potential client, he determines the value to the client of having a successful outcome. If the client needs to recover a stolen masterpiece painting, the owner asks the client what the painting is worth. The detective agency owner then sets his fee, or price, as a percentage, or fraction, of the value of the stolen painting. Because his agency is an expert in the stolen art recovery field, the agency can charge more than an hourly rate. His firm's expertise deserves a premium price, but competition is a governor on how much that premium price will be.

If the stolen art experts can find and recover a $1,000,000 painting in a minute, should they charge 1/60 of an hourly rate? Of course not.

When pricing a product, you must focus on the ultimate value the product delivers to the customer, not on the product itself. To illustrate, a company that makes household glues invented a clear adhesive that could bond and repair glass, crystal, and ceramics. The company debated internally as to what was the best pricing strategy. The traditionalists argued that superglues sold for $1.89. Thus, the glass bonding glue should sell for $1.99. The traditionalists' rationale was based on what the retailers thought was the correct price point. (Note: Retailers' opinions are important, but they are not the customer; they are a channel to the customer.) The price-to-value folks argued that the new glue should be priced at $9.99 (five times the superglue range). Their rationale was that customers for a glass bonder were not gluing jelly jars, rather they were repairing Waterford crystal goblets. Therefore, glass bonder customers were more interested in the value of the repaired goblet than they were in the price of the glue. As is the case over 90 percent of the time, the traditionalists won. The product was launched at $1.99 and was a complete flop. The customers did not believe the claim that an inexpensive glue was safe to use to repair Grandma's antique glass mirror. Later, a smarter, tougher company introduced a glass bonder, priced it at $24.99, sold it first to jewelers and antique repair stores, and sold all they could make.

A pricing-to-value mentality and philosophy forces you to focus on areas where your business can provide the greatest impact to your customers. When you find yourself selling a product that has no pricing power, you are probably offering something your customer can get anywhere. But when you can create value and price accordingly, your customer wins and your business wins. That's BIG Money!

## • XXII •
## *Sell Money, Not Products*

*C*ustomers don't buy products or services: They buy what they get from the products and services. Customers don't buy medicine, they buy cures. Customers don't buy blankets, they buy warmth. Customers don't buy gaskets, they buy non-leaking, dry engines. And warmth, cures, and leak-free engines have a monetary value delivered by the medicine, the blanket, and the gasket. Customers only buy products for two reasons: (1) to solve a problem or (2) to feel good, or some combination.

For products that solve a problem, the selling company must dollarize the value of the solution. If the dollarized value of the product is greater than its price, then price is a detail. For products that customers buy to feel good (such as a stuffed toy animal, or a contribution to a charity, or an attractive bathing suit), the customers dollarize the value. Dollarization is the way to express the value of a product's benefits in dollars and cents. For example, here is how a seller or renter of parking lot floodlights would express the value of the lights to a grocery store owner. The grocery store owner needs the lights to attract people to his store after nightfall. With a well-lit parking lot, more people will shop at the store.

The floodlight seller helps the grocer calculate the dollarized value of the lights. If the store is open six nights a week, and the lights are used in the winter months for fifteen weeks, the value of the lights is equal to the extra business generated in 90 nights. Say, every night averages twenty customers who buy $50 worth of groceries. If the average gross margin of the groceries is 35 percent, then each purchase generates $17.50 in revenues over the grocer's purchase cost of the groceries. Therefore, the lights are worth 90 nights times 20 customers times $17.50 per purchase, or $31,500 in gross margin.

The seller of the lights does not sell lights. He sells

illumination, and values that illumination at $31,500. The light seller sells money. If the grocer pays $5,000 for the lights, he generates an extra net $26,500 in gross margin dollars to use to pay bills and make profits.

Sell money, not products, and you will sell a lot of product.

## • XXIII •
## *Always Take the Business*

Get the business first, then figure out how to deliver. Get the project, get the client, get the contract, get the business. Don't let "lack of capacity" stand in the way of getting new business. Don't let "lack of people" prevent you from taking on the project. It is hard to get business. Don't make it harder by manufacturing ways to not bid, to not try, to not sign the deal. Always say yes. Always take the business.

Never turn down profitable business!

If you own a small advertising agency and you land a big new client, take the business and start looking for copywriters and account execs. If you own a small construction company and you win the job to build a school, start hiring carpenters and masons, or hire subcontracting firms that already have carpenters and masons. If you own a flower shop and can get an order to do twenty weddings, take the order. There are plenty of flowers, and plenty of florists willing to help do the job.

If you can make money on the job, always take the business. Always get the customer. There is always a way to deliver.

Always get the order! Don't lie, don't cheat, don't lose money. But don't lose the business. It is usually business lost forever.

Remember the old sales maxim: Nothing happens until somebody sells something. The small business owner always sells something . . . and often sells something he doesn't quite have.

## • XXIV •

## *Use the Leverage Levers*

*I*n a perfect business world, the small business, and the small business owner, would do nothing but sell. The small business wouldn't manufacture anything, wouldn't send bills, wouldn't fill out forms, wouldn't read and sign leases or contracts, wouldn't do any administration. The small business owner wouldn't do any such business chores because they don't add value. Such chores consume money and time.

The perfect world is unrealistic. The perfect world is probably an impossibility. But managing your business to get to the perfect world is a good guideline. The small business should only do those core activities that get and keep customers; do only those activities that give the customers what they want, when they want it.

Consequently, you must keep your business lean, lean, lean, and simple, simple, simple. Any necessary activity that you, the owner, can't do well must be done by someone else. Any function not core to your business must be done by someone else. Hiring others to do things is how you increase your span of work, how you get leverage. Archimedes wanted only one lever, but you have several. Your leverage levers include delegation, outsourcing, consultants, outside experts, temp workers, interns, retired grandfathers.

As much as possible, as much as affordable, use the leverage levers. Here is a scattergram on using the leverage levers:

1. Delegate. Assume you have three employees, and one is making $30 an hour, another $20 an hour, and the third is making $15 an hour. If all three are equally competent to do a task, delegate that task to the person making $15 an hour. Delegate as much as you can to the lowest paid employee competent enough to do the job.

**2.** Outsource. Outsourcing means moving business activities out of the company, and hiring companies that specialize in doing that activity. For example, many small businesses spend time doing bookkeeping and payroll check writing. These activities should be outsourced to people or companies whose core business is bookkeeping and payroll check writing. Other activities that should be outsourced include accounting, legal, advertising, food service, landscaping, driving (see Chapter XXV), publicity, office cleaning, mailroom. Some companies outsource their manufacturing. For example, Nike has all of its basketball sneakers manufactured by companies in Asia. Some businesses outsource secretarial help, receptionists, copy machines, and computer printers by sharing common business offices. Some companies outsource their sales function by hiring independent sales companies such as manufacturer's rep organizations or full-commissioned sales people.

**3.** Consultants. There are consultants who can provide expertise and experience in every business discipline and in every industry.

4. Temporary workers. There are armies of temp workers quite competent to handle temporary jobs, rush jobs, special jobs.

5. Interns. Intelligent, eager, hardworking, enthusiastic college and graduate students get things done if well supervised.

6. Retired grandfathers. Retirees are an untapped source of experience, expertise, and wisdom. Retirees are great workers, and are gettable at a relatively low cost. But roping in your retired grandfather is the best deal. He will help you succeed and won't charge you a cent.

Leverage yourself and your business to grow and to succeed.

## • XXV •
## *Get a Personal Driver*

You must spend your time getting and keeping customers. This means calling customers, talking to customers, visiting customers, writing proposals, writing advertising copy to get customers, writing and e-mailing to customers, reading about your customers. Any activity that robs you of your customer-getting time robs your business. Driving is a time thief. If you have a business that causes you to often spend long periods of time in a car (two hours or more per trip), get a personal driver(s).

Having a driver frees you to talk to and write to customers, suppliers, employees. Having a driver lets you safely (and legally) dial numbers, pay attention to customers, and take notes. Having a driver extends your workday because you can continue to work after nightfall. (Get a car desk with an attached night lamp.) Having a driver reduces stress and hassle, making you more productive. Having a driver is safer: The driver is not preoccupied with non-driving activities, and is not tired. Having a driver saves driving time. You don't have to find streets, locations, parking spaces. You don't have to wait for a taxi. You can be dropped at the international terminal instead of schlepping your bags two miles from a parking garage. You can be dropped directly at your appointment. Having a driver saves money. A driver often eliminates parking fees, cab costs, rental car charges. The hourly wage to a driver will be less than your pay (if not true at the outset of your business, it will be ultimately). If it costs $20 an hour for your driver, and your time is worth $25 an hour, then you make $5 for every hour someone else drives. Conversely, if you drive, you lose $25 for every hour you drive.

There are many retired people willing to be drivers. There are part-time workers willing to be drivers. They like the diversion, and they like the extra money. An ad in your local paper will generate good candidates. You will find that good drivers are well-mannered, well-read, safe, presentable, and dependable. Have a pool of drivers, to ensure availability, and sometimes, in periods of extensive driving, to ensure having a well-rested driver.

Driving your car (which should be a company car because you own the small business) keeps costs down, as you pay the driver only for his or her time and do not pay for wear and tear on his or her car. Your car expense, lease payments, maintenance, and fuel are a constant—regardless of who drives your car. Your car expense is a company expense and deductible. So, have your driver drive your car.

Some businesses bill clients for expenses. Keeping your customer's expenses down is good business—it leaves more money in the client's budget to pay you for more services. The travel expense for a driver is usually the lowest travel expense option

Having a driver is not a luxury for the small business owner. Having a driver is not frivolous. Having a driver gives you more time to work, more time to get and keep customers. So when he is driving you someplace, you are driving your business to a better place.

## • XXVI •
## *"What if He Had Died?"*

*I*n small businesses there are no extra employees. There are no major league players sitting on the bench waiting to play, to go to work. There is no backup team. In a small business every employee is doing the work and tasks that must be done. Everyone is working, and is working hard. In a small company every employee is integral to the success of the enterprise.

Every employee is to a small business similar to what an automotive part is to a car: What's more important to driving a car . . . the spark plugs, the steering wheel, the motor? You can't drive the car if one of the key parts is missing. Correspondingly, the small business without all its parts, like a spark-plug-deprived auto, does not run smoothly. It stops, it swerves, it idles. To extend this agonizing auto analogy, some parts in a car, and in a company, are hard or easy to replace, expensive or less expensive, readily available or rare. It may be harder, take longer, cost more to replace a trained technician than a trained truck driver.

Because the well-run small business is so leanly staffed, losing an employee is usually upsetting. (One exception is the planned retirement of an employee.) It is especially traumatic if the loss of the employee is sudden, unplanned. Sudden loss would be the case if an employee had to be fired immediately (say for committing theft), or if an employee quits.

"What if he had died?" is a hypothetical question. It is the question to ask yourself when you consider the implications of possibly losing a key employee sometime in the future. It is the question to ask yourself when you suddenly lose an employee for whatever reason. It is the question to ask when an employee quits.

It is often unexpected when an employee quits. There is rarely a contingency plan. Unexpected surprises can throw the harried and overly stretched business owner into a frazzle. If the resignation is tinged with discordant personality issues, as is often the case, emotions can affect judgment. The small business owner needs to immediately get past the quitting and get into action. You, the small business owner, must stop, think, think clearly, and solve the problem.

The question "What if he had died?" depersonalizes the event. The question takes the emotion out of the situation and grounds the company owner. The question closes the door on the immediate past and mentally frees the small business owner to go forward. The small business owner has no choice but to keep going. There is always a solution.

The question "What if he had died?" is challenging. The question is cold. When you ask the question of yourself, you immediately know that hand-wringing and mopitry are not acceptable reactions. You know you have to do something. Maybe you can get a temporary employee. Maybe you can outsource to a freelancer or consultant. Maybe you can corral someone you know who is lollygagging on a beach and put her back to work. Or maybe you will have to go back to working eighteen hours a day . . . for a while. You've done it before. Maybe you will work all night. You don't care! You are the owner of your small business!

What if he had died? You can't care. You have customers to sell, to serve. You have a business to run. Get on with it.

# · XXVII ·
## *Inoculate Against FTD*

$S$ TD stands for "sexually transmitted disease." FTD stands for "financially transmitted disease." Both syndromes are hard to cure, or are incurable, or are fatal. FTD only infects employees. Symptoms include one employee's jealousy over another employee's compensation; jealousy over another employee's promotion; jealousy of how much money the owner is supposedly making; telling other employees that everyone is getting ripped off by the owner. An FTD is most often caused by incorrect speculation as to who is making how much money. The speculation can be based on the cars people drive, the homes they have, the clothes they wear, the cigars they smoke.

An FTD can be caused when an employee deliberately, or by accident, gets knowledge of confidential financial information. An FTD can be caused when a senior employee, with legitimate access to the company's financial information, breaks the company's trust and lets the financial information infect and disease his or her mind and allegiance.

Employees with an FTD can rarely be cured. Giving them more money is not the right medicine. More money proves to the employee that he was right, that he always deserved to get a bigger slice of the speculative riches. Employees with an FTD gripe to other employees. They gripe and complain at home. They bad-mouth the company to friends, some of whom are customers or potential customers of the small business. You cannot allow or afford to have a financially transmitted disease spread to others. You can't have a Typhoid Mary or a Herpes Harry in your company. You must not allow one employee to start an epidemic.

His name was Arnold. He was a trusted employee. He had to be trustworthy because he was the director of finance for a forty-seven-person manufacturing company. He was privy to salaries, profits, perquisites. He knew who made how much money. For several years Arnold seemed content with his compensation, which was not only fair, but considering the employee's background and job duties, was generous, hard to match in the marketplace. Recently, he started sending signals to his boss, the owner of the manufacturing company, that he felt underpaid, underappreciated, and deserved a promotion. Although Arnold voiced his concerns only to his boss when in the company, outside the office he stewed and fumed.

He complained bitterly to his friends and his wife. What particularly galled and irked Arnold was the amount of money the owner was taking out of the company. Arnold told his wife that the owner was working less, paying himself more, charging the company exorbitant rent for the company's building (which the boss owned), and was constructing a fabulous summer home. Arnold's wife poured jet fuel on her husband's fire.

Arnold's wife said, "Joe would never have the business he has without you. You gave him the best years of your life. You should be making more money. You should give Joe an ultimatum: no more pay, no more stay. He coughs up more money, or you're out of there.

And tell Joe to get rid of that punk sales manager. Even he makes more money than you." And his wife never stopped. Every night she needled and complained.

Both Arnold and his wife conveniently forgot that they never missed a paycheck. They forgot that Joe often went unpaid to meet payroll. They forgot all the loans for which Joe personally signed. Arnold and his wife were sick with a bad case of FTD.

The inevitable happened. Arnold met with his boss, and asked for a pay raise that would have doubled his cash compensation over two years. Arnold said that he had been comparing salaries in the area; that he had been given advice by an outside firm; and that he was clearly the most important person in the forty-seven-person company. Joe was thunderstruck but never flinched, never showed emotion. Joe told his employee that a doubling of compensation was absurd, a nonstarter. Arnold told Joe the new compensation package was fair and deserved. Arnold then said, "Let's face it, Joe—you can afford it. Look at all the money you are grabbing."

Two days later, after consulting with his attorney and advisors, Joe had a forty-six-person company. FTD kills.

To prevent the spread of FTD, terminate the infected employee. Terminate the transmitter. Getting rid of disease is one way to keep your small business healthy.

## • XXVIII •
## *Never Run Out of Cash*

C ash is money in the bank. Cash also is cash equiv-
alents, which are highly liquid investments such
as stock and money market funds. Cash is a company's
oxygen. Cash keeps the company going. Cash is more
important than profits. A company can have cash, and
no profits, and keep going. A company with profits but
no cash is in big trouble.

Cash comes from collecting accounts receivable,
collecting what customers owe. Cash comes from
stretching out accounts payable, keeping cash in the
company by paying bills slowly. Cash comes from investors and sources of credit. Cash comes from selling

assets. Having cash allows a company to avoid borrowing money, thereby reducing interest costs. With cash, the small business can take advantage of unexpected bargain purchase opportunities. Cash allows a company to take purchase discounts by paying early. Cash is used to pay bonuses and dividends.

Every work morning, the first thing the owner of a small maritime shipping company does is to check his company's cash position. He then looks at his cash needs. He subtracts cash needs from cash. He then knows if he needs to tap into his line of bank credit. His company's revenues are highly predictable because the ships are booked into long-term contracts. Cash is needed to pay the crews, pay anchorage, docking, and port fees. Consequently, keeping costs down, and matching cash to cash needs, are important drivers for his company's profitability.

Try to have enough cash on hand that is equivalent to two months of company expenses. This is often hard to do, but it is a good cash goal.

Never let your company run out of cash.

Cash is treasure. Treasure cash.

## • XXIX •
### *Patent, Protect, and Padlock*

There is a reality called "competitive intelligence"
or "business espionage." There are businesses
that specialize in "competitive intelligence," "reverse
engineering," or the banal phrase "market research."
These businesses exist to find out everything about the
small business owner—the business's plans, its technology, its people, its everything. These investigative
firms are mostly law-abiding. They don't need to do
anything illegal, as it is so easy to find out what most
companies are about simply by observing, asking, and
listening. Some unsavory investigative firms bribe, lie,
and scuttle through trash. Whatever the means, the

end is to understand, neutralize, or eliminate your company's edge in the marketplace.

Patent what you can. If you can't patent an innovation or discovery or insight, make it a "trade secret," and keep it secret. The Coca-Cola Co.'s formula for Coca-Cola is a one-hundred-year-old trade secret. Competitors have tried unsuccessfully for decades to replicate the unique taste of Beefeater gin. But the recipe to make Beefeater gin is under lock and key in some dungeon in England. For 400 years the Zildjian family has been making cymbals, those exquisite musical instruments that make a marching band, and a rock and roll drummer a rocker. The family's secret to manufacturing wonderful cymbals is a closely guarded metallurgy formulation.

If something is of value to you, it is valuable to your competitors. Patent all innovations and inventions. Trademark all brands and slogans. Put proprietary formulae and processes and machinery designs in a padlocked vault. Don't let anyone know your "Black Box." If you have a way to do something easier or faster or less expensively than your competitors, don't tell anyone. Don't brag about your special expertise. Keep quiet.

Brand names are intellectual assets of often priceless value. The Coca-Cola Co. lost the proprietary use of the word *cola* (as in RC Cola and Pepsi-Cola) in the early 1900s. They have never lost another brand. A Coca-Cola internal intellectual asset protection department of over fifty lawyers makes certain. Coke is a fiercely protected brand name. The unique color and shape of the classic $6\frac{1}{2}$-ounce green Coca-Cola bottle is protected under trademark law.

Depending on your assessment of the value of your secrets or technology, hire security experts to protect and plug all leaks in computer systems, e-mail, document proliferation, file storage. Put video cameras where needed. Depending on the sensitivity of your designs and data and marketing edge, be sure you can trust all of your people all of the time. Unfortunately, a trustworthy person in employment years one to five can be co-opted or corrupted in year ten. Stay vigilant. To stay alert, and to honor the great songwriter Johnny Cash, sing to yourself one of Johnny Cash's memorable lines: "I keep my eyes wide open all the time."

There are new federal white-collar crime laws that protect business owners against the theft of intellectual property. The law is called the Economic Espionage Act. The law is sweeping. For example, the theft of a company's internal telephone directory puts the thief at dire risk. The penalties are draconian. People convicted of violating these laws can be levied triple financial damages or jail time, or both. These laws are to white-collar crime as the RICO statutes are to racketeering. Be sure all your employees are aware of these laws and of the consequences of breaking them.

Keeping secrets is often the secret of success.

## • XXX •
## *Have Regular B & P Meetings*

*B* stands for billing. *P* means pricing. Hold frequent billing and pricing meetings. One purpose of the B & P is to make sure you are properly billing. Proper billing means billing fast; billing for all products and services the customer agreed to or bought; billing for all the little items and incidentals. It is easy to forget to bill a legitimate charge. It is easy to misbill or late bill. Billing is a critical administrative task, and because it is administrative, it can take a back seat to other urgent company matters. Don't let billing be anything but important. B & P meetings eliminate the tendency to accumulate charges and "bill once a month." Bill daily if

services, and everyone works to produce the designs and prints.

Regardless of the structure, marketing must talk to manufacturing constantly. Marketing is always thinking, "How do we sell more?" Manufacturing is always thinking, "How do we make what marketing sells?" Marketing must tell manufacturing about projects sold, pending orders, upcoming sales-producing promotions, new products, new packaging concepts in the pipeline. Manufacturing needs this information to plan how it will meet demand. Manufacturing needs to plan for capacity, manpower, material, inventory, parts, PowerPoint presentations, report binding, or whatever it takes to produce and deliver the product or service.

Marketing and manufacturing must know each function's planning requirements, limits, problems. The two functions must work with each other to understand forecasts, product costs, pricing, delivery date promises, product quality issues, product returns, production possibilities and impossibilities. Production impossibilities are much rarer in companies that are focused on serving a finite, understood set of customer needs, than they are in companies that are all over the place. If your small business is organized to paint residential homes, then you probably are not able to paint lines and curbs in a major shopping center's parking lot.

Sellers and makers work for the same boss . . . the customer. Sellers and makers have at least one common goal: giving customers what they want, when they want it. If marketing and sales people are voicing problems with manufacturing, it is marketing's problem. If manufacturing is voicing problems with sales, it is manufacturing's problem. Make the two functions talk to each other to make the problems go away.

Heed the agreement made between Ernest and Julio Gallo, two of the titans in the wine business. They made this agreement when the E&J Gallo Winery had only two employees, and kept it as they grew their company into a giant. Ernest, the marketing genius, was responsible for sales; Julio, the winemaker, was responsible for producing the wine. Their agreement: Ernest Gallo would sell all the wine that Julio Gallo could make, and Julio would make all the wine Ernest could sell.

Sell it. Make it. Deliver it. Bill it. Get paid for it.

## • XXXII •

# The Business Owner Is Not the Boss

Y ou may own the company, but you are not the boss. You may be the only employee, but you are not the boss. You have many bosses.

Your first boss is your customer. You work for the customer. The good customer tells you what she wants and you do it. If the customer wants polished apples, polish the apples. If the customer asks for a weekly update, schedule time every Friday. If the customer wants to pay with an American Express card, accept the American Express card. You do whatever your profitable, good customer wants.

You work for your employees. You remove barriers that frustrate them from doing a good job. You train employees. You make their job and their workplace and their life richer and better. You listen to the employees and act on their good ideas.

You may have lenders or investors or partners. You have obligations to do for them what you have promised. You have to give them a return on their money. You may have signed contracts, such as a store lease. You are obligated.

The small business owner has to deal with a bewildering dust storm of laws and regulations and tax requirements. Far too many government-imposed regulations are restrictive, anti-competitive, expensive, and stupid, but they exist, and they collectively are a big, bad boss.

Everyone thinks you are the boss, but now you know better. And if you ever catch yourself about to say to a stubborn employee, or to a mystifyingly unreliable supplier, something akin to, "Hey, I'm the boss around here," stop. Don't say it. To say "I am the boss" means you have lost your authority. Employees and suppliers know you are the boss.

You work for your customers. You work for your

employees, and lenders, and stockholders. And you work for the tax man. But you also are working for yourself, and you are worth it.

## • XXXIII •
## *Always Take Contemporaneous Notes*

*C* ontemporaneous notes are those notes one takes during, or immediately after, a telephone call or meeting with a customer, supplier, troublesome employee, or anyone part of an important issue. Contemporaneous notes are part of the paper trail. They are critical reference information indespensible in disputes, negotiations, reconstructing billing records, proposal development. They are invaluable in recreating a situation that happened in the past, particularly if all or some of the participants are no longer around.

Contemporaneous notes can be accepted as evidence in civil suits. They are especially effective if the notes are co-signed or co-initialed by another party. These notes often contain what might be considered mundane observations or trivial facts. However, the utter triviality of a fact gives the notes power. Little things, specific facts, specific quotes, give the notes credibility and legitimacy. Keep credible contemporaneous notes.

John Smith was a successful carpenter. He was a sole proprietor. He built and remodeled houses, and hired subcontractors to do the work he didn't do personally. He was a careful, organized man who kept a detailed work diary. He used the diary to record expenses for taxes, to keep his accounts in order, to record when he ordered materials, to track hours worked. In his diary, John Smith kept contemporaneous notes on conversations with suppliers, subcontractors, bankers, real estate people, and customers.

A customer of Smith's declared that Smith had not performed as agreed and refused to pay. The money at issue was considerable. The customer was wealthy and figured he could outspend (on lawyers) and outlast Smith in a lawsuit. There was no formal contract, just a pre-job estimate by Smith. Smith sued. It was eight months later that Smith's lawsuit was in the courts.

The lawsuit was brought before a judge, one experienced in civil lawsuits. Smith felt he could not afford a lawyer and hoped the judge would understand.

When on the stand, Smith was asked a question by one of the lawyers. Before answering, Smith casually asked the judge if he could refer to his notes. Somewhat surprised, the judge asked, "You have notes? What kind of notes?" Smith told the judge about his diary, and pulled a well-worn little black book from his work jacket. Smith's black book, his contemporaneous notes, detailed all construction expenditures, all requests from the customer, changes made by the customers, everything that was done on the job. The judge reviewed the notes and admitted them as evidence. Instead of a "his word versus his word" argument, Smith now had evidence. The judge ruled in Smith's favor, awarding Smith the original sum of money, interest, legal fees, and a punitive award.

Contemporaneous notes won that lawsuit.

There is a rule in the advertising business: If it's not written down, it doesn't exist. Heed this rule in your own small business. Keep important e-mails. If it is legal, tape-record meetings, or tape your thoughts before and after meetings or phone calls. Tape your side of a conversation. Make copies of handwritten notes you send, and keep on file. Don't tell anyone you keep contemporaneous notes. If you never need the notes, that is great. But if you do, they can save you a great deal of money. The taking of contemporaneous notes is an absolute must for the small business owner. They may save you.

Note today that which you may need tomorrow.

## • XXXIV •

## *You Are Working When You Are Not Working*

*A*s a small business owner you are the embodiment of your company. You are the custodian of your company's name and image in the marketplace. And the marketplace is everywhere! Everyone and anyone you meet, or who observes you, can be a potential customer or someone who can influence a potential customer.

Always be mindful that you are constantly selling your company. You are always in view. Therefore, you must always be on guard as to how you act.

Don't scream at the ref at your kid's soccer game; he or she could be a prospective customer. Don't run someone off the road; he might be the banker you're supposed to meet tomorrow.

Don't be like the boorish sales manager from Cleveland, flying first class to Connecticut for a job interview with the owner of a successful small business. The job candidate was in row three. In row one was a man in his forties, traveling with his elderly father.

When the plane landed, the fellow in row one helped his father get ready to deplane. The old gent was a little slow. The guy from Cleveland, impatient and rude, scolded in a loud voice, "C'mon, move it!" The jibe was doubly unnecessary as the Cleveland traveler was seen minutes later waiting for bags at the luggage carousel.

The next day the prospective sales manager was introduced to the small business owner. The job interview lasted only a few minutes. The small business owner was seated in row four on the same flight as the man from Cleveland.

The sales manager didn't know he was applying for the job while he was flying. He didn't know that he was supposed to act like a sales manager: selling, leading, setting an example, making friends, not making enemies. If he had helped the older fellow with his bag, he would have been closer to getting the job.

Later the small business owner remarked that he was glad he observed the incident. He felt he ducked a bullet. He was also amazed that the sales manager acted the way he did while wearing his company jacket with the company name in big red letters. The owner said, "Rude and dumb: a deadly combination."

You are always working.

# Never Let Anyone Outwork You

You may not be the smartest. You may not have the most talent. You may be disorganized or dyslexic or dingy. You may not have a lot of things your competition has. Plus, you have little or no control over the competition. If you own a beachside hot dog stand, you can't make it stop raining. If you own a ski lodge, you can't make it start snowing If you own a company that exports or imports, you can't change the currency valuations.

There is one thing you can do: You can work. You can out plan, outhustle, outsell, and outwork anybody. You can make one more sales call. You can write one more proposal. You can rearrange the merchandise. You can try a new sales promotion. You can have a midnight sale. You can write a new commercial, put up a new sign, refinance your loans, spruce up the waiting room, put in a new menu, call every prospect in your Rolodex. You can open sooner or close later. You can write an article. Send out a press release.

This is a story about a neighborhood in a city where one "new" poor ethnic set of grocers outworked an established, well-off "old" ethnic set of grocers. The established grocers had big, beautiful successful stores. The new grocers could barely afford the ratty little dumps that would become their grocery stores. Most of the founding owners of the established stores had passed the business down through generations, or sold their stores to big chains. The old grocers were open from 8:00 A.M. to 8:00 P.M. The new grocers opened at 6:00 A.M. and closed at 11:00 P.M., or later if customers stopped by. The new grocers delivered bags of food to customers. The heirs or buyers of the original grocery stores did not deliver; to them the cost was prohibitive. The new grocers charged five cents more for every product that was fresher, colder, warmer, or only available in their store. The established grocers cut prices, offered lots of coupons, offered super shopper savers, all of which cut margins and profits. The new grocers worked long hours, rented or bought the apartments above their stores and lived there, and put all their energy and time and money into making each rare new customer a repeat customer. When the new ethnic invasion was over, and the old grocers were gone, the plaintive wail from one grandson who ran one of the vanquished stores said it all: "C'mon, ᵖ. Don't blame me. These people work eighteen a day. What could I do?" "Pop," who was eighty- rs old and from the "old country," looked at his and answered, "Work twenty hours."

always do something! It may not work, but d if you are working, good things *might* you are outworking the other guy, good n.

re working and not just in motion. Chair Syndrome" (the person in e crazy but going nowhere). Do npact.

rking on something in your mething that comes easy to do not take it easy. Bril- he other songwriters. lian painters. Raphael out frescoed the entire Renaissance. To paraphrase part of the Protestant work ethic: If it's not hard work, you are letting something slide.

If you have to work to win, then never, ever, let the other guy outwork you.

## · XXXVI ·

## Work on the Business, Not Just in the Business

Working *in* the business is doing everything that needs getting done. For example, if you own a dry cleaning company, working in the business means bundling customers' clothes, printing a pickup slip, cleaning clothes, pressing pants, boxing shirts, wiping the counter, shoveling the sidewalk, collecting money, paying suppliers, locking the door at night. Many small business owners, at the start, spend 100 percent of their time working in the business. They may not have any employees, any help. They have to do everything needed to get the business going, and to keep it going. Working in the business is what must be done to learn the business, and to get the business to where it can grow.

Working *on* the business is planning the future, planning management succession, selecting great employees, training employees, assigning and delegating tasks to employees, introducing and trying new products and services, arranging financing, looking for new markets, building a larger facility. Working *on* the business requires study, thinking, planning, not just doing.

The owner of the dry cleaning company worked hard, and worked long hours. His business was successful: He had a good location, good product, good marketplace. His dilemma was that he could not grow his business to meet customer demand, primarily, although he did not know it, because he was still working in the business. He was still pressing slacks, still finding misplaced clothes, still writing every advertisement. Upon advice, he relented and hired a store manager. He struggled to find the time to train the new store manager. He struggled to delegate, to give up everyday tasks. But after one month the company was doing greater volume, customer service had improved, and the owner had time to begin active preparation to open a second dry cleaning store. And the first act for the new store was hiring a store manager.

There are barriers that hinder the business owner from working on the business instead of in the business. The owner may feel that no one else can do the job as well as she can. If true, the business will only be as big as the owner's personal work capacity. The owner may feel she can't afford to bring on employees . . . to do more of what she was doing. The owner may feel she doesn't have the time to do anything but what she is doing.

These are legitimate issues, but if the small business owner wants to make more money, she must find a way to get lower value work activities done by lower paid workers. She must invest time and money into productivity, improving people or technology or both.

## *Strike Out Often*

*L*ike great scorers in athletics, it is not the number of shots you miss that counts, it is the number of shots you make that counts. In baseball, even the best hitters make outs twice as often as they get hits. No one cares how many times Seabiscuit lost a race. Don't worry about losing. Don't despair if you make a mistake. Analyze your attempt, and use what you learn to plan your next attempt. And don't hesitate to do it again.

It is not the number of failed sales calls that rings the cash register, it is the number of successful sales calls that makes money.

One successful sales call can save the company. So don't let failed sales calls prevent you from making the next sales call.

It is not the number of houses you show to a client that matters; it is the house she buys that pays your commission. If you don't show enough houses, you lose. It is not the number of customers who walk out without buying that pays your bills, it is those who buy that do.

Don't apply, and you won't get in. Don't make the loan, and you won't get the interest. Don't try the recipe, you won't sell the dish. Don't swing the bat, you won't get a hit. You can't win it if you are not in it.

Strikeouts are good. They mean you went to the plate, that you visited a customer, that you tried something to help the business. Lots of strikeouts mean lots of attempts. And there are never enough attempts. Don't stop doing what you have to do until you get it done.

Realize that no one does everything right every time. Realize that strikeouts are part of the game. Realize that rejection is part of the business game. Even the best salespeople, the rainmakers, get rejected. Don't get dejected because you were rejected. Don't drop out because you struck out. Don't hang your head. Don't despair. Repair. Prepare. Try again . . . and again.

Give yourself time. Be patient. It is harder to succeed at the start than later. But be realistic. If you are not getting better, if what you are doing simply won't work, ask your customers and prospects for reaction, for clues to succeed. Then do what the customers say.

It is okay to strike out often. It is not okay to strike out always.

## • XXXVIII •
### *Stay Off Boards and Committees*

*B*ecause you are a small business owner you will, in your community, be perceived as financially successful and, maybe, thought to be smart. You will be a prospect to sit on the boards of not-for-profit organizations. These organizations are worthy, and typically are involved in the theater, education, health services, opera, museums, charities. The people who run these organizations want only one thing from you: They want money. They may appreciate your business acumen, but they want your money first. They actually need your business experience big time, and some proactively seek your advice, but getting your donations is their primary interest.

The not-so-secret rule for what is expected from board members is: "Give, get, or get off." That is, "Give money; get money; or get your butt off the board." You will be much better off, and just as appreciated, if you give money and do not join the board.

Regardless of the worthiness of the organization, you do not have the time to prepare for and attend meetings. Because you are conscientious, you will steal time from your business, frittering it away as a board member. Conserve your time. Give money instead.

There are exceptions to the "no boards" rule, but these exceptions are allowed only after the ten-year anniversary of your company's startup date. Consider joining a board . . .

- If membership on the board will directly lead to new business for your company without compromising the integrity of your membership.
- If you are passionate about an organization or a cause.

- If board membership is prestigious, and membership will help your business.
- If the organization is critical to the well-being of your community, and your membership will positively affect the community.
- If you are giving something back to the organization, for example helping the college that gave you a scholarship.

One board membership at a time is plenty. Two memberships is absolutely the maximum.

Don't join the board of any industry associations. If your small business is in an industry that has an association for all members, such as the National Association of Electrical Wholesalers, do not join that industry's board, or go on any committees. Go to the annual association meetings if you will learn something. At the meetings just listen and learn. Don't talk.

And don't run for your local board of selectmen or zoning board of appeals. These worthy offices will devour your calendar.

Invest your time in your family, yourself, your life, your business. It is okay to coach your kid's soccer team. Coaching is fun and you are investing in your family. Hoard your time. Invest it where the returns are real.

On polite boards, directors or trustees are asked to give "wealth *or* wisdom." But the real request is "wealth *and* wisdom." There is no option. If you have no wisdom, giving your wealth will be fine.

No boards. No committees. No clubs. No organizations. No memberships means more time to make money.

## • XXXIX •

## *Always Keep the C's Top of Mind*

There are a million things to think about when you are a business owner, but some things are paramount. Remember the C's and constantly keep them at the top of your mind.

- C for "customer." Without a paying customer, your business will fail.
- C for "cash." You must never run out of cash.
- C for "collection." Collect the cash.
- C for "credit." Credit becomes cash.
- C for "costs." Don't waste money. Keep costs down. Cut unnecessary costs.

- C for "closing," as in closing orders or closing sales.
- C for "confidence." Everyone likes winners.
- C for "calm." No matter how bad it gets; no matter how traumatic; no matter the trouble, tell yourself, "Be calm," and you will.
- C for "commitment." You started the business—never quit!

## · XL ·

# *Get Today's Technology, but Wait Until Tomorrow*

You must invest in technology (new products) that save time, reduce costs, increase worker productivity, help get customers. But don't be the first to invest. Wait until the bugs are fixed and the costs come down. You will not lose an advantage by waiting. Rather, you will avoid the stress, downtime, work interruptions, and distractions that are always a part of the learning curve required to master new technology.

Let the big, slow-moving corporations buy the newest sales automation system. Let the big innovation-bereft corporations grasp the newest project management software as they vainly attempt to get as nimble as small businesses. Let the other guys prove out the new technology.

Invest in technology you will use. Don't buy functions and applications you don't need. Have simple expectations and simple objectives for what the technology will do. Don't overcomplicate things. If the new product can reduce costs, improve quality, please customers, and do so with an absolute minimum of hassle, get it. But be sure you are not the early adopter.

Avoid technology that supposedly reduces costs, but distances you or your employees from the customer. For example, try to call your national phone company for residential service repair or your direct TV company to solve any problem. You will be politely, courteously sent spinning into cyberspace by some auto-voice.

If technology is great, it is worth the wait. So wait.

# XLI

# *Sign 500 Holiday Cards*

*H*olidays are an occasion to send a message to customers and prospects. Take advantage of the occasion. At Christmastime sign and send 500 cards. Be sensitive to the religious beliefs of the person to whom you are sending a card so as not to offend. Or, at Thanksgiving sign and send 400 cards (to U.S. celebrants) and don't worry about offending the turkeys. Or, send Halloween cards, and if you want to scare your customers, include your picture.

Send unusual, distinctive, memorable, tasteful cards. Personally sign every card. Do not send unsigned cards or cards that are preprinted with your company's name or your name. Don't send e-mail cards. Don't just sign your name. Use the card as a marketing tool to sell. Add a personal note to every card. Suggest lunch. Handwrite your telephone number. Write in your e-mail address. Tastefully, politely, gently, but specifically, remind the customer to put money in his next year's budget for your company.

Holidays are good times to communicate with your customers. The small business owner never takes a holiday from selling.

# XLII

# Give "Surprizes"

Customers love getting more than they paid for. Customers love getting something "for free." Customers love getting a nice surprise. Customers love the restaurateur who occasionally sends over a drink "on the house." Customers love the Cancun, Mexico, resort hotel that leaves a new and different seashell by the pillow each night. Customers love the haberdasher who slips a pocket silk into the breast of a recently purchased suit. Customers love the car wash that gives their dog a dog cookie. Customers love being treated as special.

So, give surprizes. Give your customers surprise prizes.

Cracker Jack built its brand with its famous "surprise inside." McDonald's toy promotions sell millions of "Happy Meals." With its terrific watches and other surprises, Lucky Charms cereal has become a sensation with the teenage market.

Customers love getting a little extra. Customers love doing business with companies that are full of fun surprises. Be like the hairdressing salon in Farmington, Connecticut, that lets each customer leave with a single red rose. The pharmacist who calls a mother to inquire about her child's fever stands out, and gets all of that mom's prescriptions. That's marketing. That's loving your customers, loving your company, and building your business.

Surprise your customer, and surprise, surprise: You will keep that customer. Customers are the source of BIG money.

# Small Business Owner's Daily To-Do List

- Exercise.
- Reach out to new customers.
- Contact existing customers.
- Sell to existing customers.
- Achieve one important objective.
- Execute a marketing event.
- Do one important task.
- Train an employee.
- Listen to all employees. Talk to them.
- Inspect product quality.
- Inspect work on delegated tasks.

- Review progress to goals.
- Return all calls.

# XLIV

# A New Business Description

$T$he new business idea is to start a fitness and exercise center for people born between the years
1945 and 1960. It will be called Bods for Boomers.
There are sixty million or more U.S. "baby boomers."
Bods for Boomers will fill a different need from the
service now offered in most exercise facilities. Bods
for Boomers will be positioned as a place where one
need not have a perfect body, nor aspire to get one.
The customers will be older. Although there will be
common rooms, where customers can buy food, beverages, and products, the exercise facilities will be seg-
regated into men only and women only. Customers

need not worry about how they look to the opposite sex. Customers will be able to choose from a wide assortment of preprinted fitness outcomes and relevant workout programs. For example, there will be programs for weight loss, muscle strengthening, cardiovascular improvement. Each customer is on his or her own. There will be no dues or membership fees. Customers will pay for minutes used in the exercise rooms. The price is fifty cents a minute. The workout time will be started and monitored by an electronic entry/exit card. The bill will be charged to a credit card on file. Customers can schedule time or walk in. There will be separate individual shower and dressing rooms. Bods for Boomers will be located in low-cost, hard-to-rent buildings such as older shopping centers and obsolete warehouses. Facility personnel will be hired for their customer service skills, not for their physicality. "It's your body, baby. Baby your bod at Bods for Boomers."

# XLV

# You Must Know Your Breakeven(s) (Part 1)

You must know how much dollar revenue you will need to cover all your costs—to break even—in one year, or in one month, or in any time period. You must know how many units of product you must sell at what price, to break even, in one year, or in any given time period. You must know how many buying customers you will need (at some average purchase amount) per year, to break even. You need to know these breakevens before you start your small business. If you know your breakevens, you can judge whether or not you can get enough paying customers to pay your bills. You can judge if your prices should be changed. If you don't know your breakeven, you won't have the basic measurement system to manage your business. You won't know if success or failure is in front of you.

Breakeven is that dollar revenue amount when a number of customers times the average dollar gross margin per purchase per customer is equal to the total cost of doing business. Gross margin is the product selling price, after paying sales commissions, and minus material, labor, and direct overhead to make the products; or the product net selling price minus the acquisition cost of the product; or the service selling price minus the direct cost of providing the service.

For example, assume you make quilts and sell each quilt for $100. Your gross margin is based on the selling price of $100 minus the cost of the cloth patches, thread, labor, and any sales commissions. If the cloth costs you $15 per quilt, the thread costs $1, the sewing labor is $20, and you pay a 10 percent sales commission, or $10, your total production cost is $46. Your gross margin in dollars is $54 ($100 selling price minus direct production costs of $46). Your gross margin *percentage* is 54 percent ($54 divided by $100), or gross margin dollars divided by the selling price.

Next you add up all the costs of doing business for

one year. These costs include rent, utilities, advertising, insurance, some depreciation costs of the sewing machines (which your accountant will calculate), telephone, postage, vehicle cost, your desired salary or compensation, and all other costs. Assume these costs total to $50,000 for the entire year. To determine your breakeven in revenues, divide the $50,000 by your average gross margin percentage (54 percent). Your breakeven revenue is $92,600. You must sell enough quilts to generate $92,600 in sales.

To determine the breakeven in terms of quilts, divide your gross margin dollars per quilt ($54) into $50,000. Your breakeven number of quilts to sell, at $100 per quilt, is 926 quilts.

To determine the breakeven in terms of how many paying, buying customers are needed, you make assumptions. You should have done some research on quilt buyers, or have some knowledge, or both. Your research indicates that 50 percent of quilt buyers purchase three quilts at one time, and the other 50 percent buy one quilt. After doing the math, you conclude you need 464 customers who will buy one quilt, and you need 154 customers who will buy three.

Knowing your breakevens, you can better judge if the market is big enough for you to sell 926 quilts. You can better judge if you can land 618 customers; 464 who will buy one quilt, and 154 who will buy three quilts, each at $100 per quilt.

If you are sufficiently certain you can sell more than 926 quilts, go for it. If you are certain you cannot, then don't.

When you sell quilt number 10,000, have a sign made: "The House That Quilts Built."

# · XLVI ·
## *Calculating Breakevens (Part 2)*

In the previous chapter, you learned how to calculate breakevens if you are selling one product. Most small businesses sell many products and services. For example, convenience stores and grocery stores sell hundreds of products. Record stores and bookstores sell hundreds of products. Dentists sell dozens of services and procedures. When you are selling several different products at different prices with different costs, you must use an average gross margin percentage to determine your breakevens. (There are computer programs that can calculate fairly accurate gross margin percentages, but absent that, use best estimates.)

Many industries have trade magazines and industry associations that freely publish data on average gross margins, and on numerous other measurement numbers. Suppliers to small businesses can sometimes offer advice on gross margin percentages.

Determining the breakeven for a small business that sells many products or services is simple: Divide total fixed costs by the average gross margin percentage of all the products. For example, if you own a tire replacement business and if your total annual costs are $250,000, and your average gross margin percentage is 25 percent, your breakeven revenues are $1,000,000 ($250,000 divided by 25 percent). (If you are not sure of your average gross margin percentage, use a range, in this example from 20 percent to 30 percent.)

To determine the number of customers you need to attract and get to your tire company, divide your breakeven revenue amount by the average dollar purchase of each customer. If the average tire purchase is $200, then you will need 5,000 customers buying once, or 5,000 transactions, to breakeven . . . to hit $1,000,000 in revenues (5,000 purchases times $200 per purchase).

Determining breakevens is a must, and is usually simple to do. Getting to breakeven is a must, but is usually hard to do.

Now you know how many customers you need. So go get those customers.

# • XLVII •
## *Calculate the Size of Your Market*

Your market is that number of customers that you can realistically and profitably identify, attract, get, and keep. Your market, your customers, are found in your trading area. Your trading area is geographical, and might be local, regional, national, or international, or any combination.

Here are five simple steps to help you calculate the size of your market.

For example, you are opening a child-care center.

*One,* determine how many children, say, age one through five, live in your chosen trading area. That number of kids represents your hypothetical total number of customers. (The kids' parents would represent your primary marketing target.)

*Two,* reduce the pool of customers by subtracting those kids who, for whatever reason, are unlikely to go to a day-care center. Go to the town halls in your trading area and find that there are 5,000 kids aged one through five. You read industry articles and do a small parent survey, and determine that 60 percent of the children in your trading area will not use day care and 40 percent will. Therefore, your potential customer base is 2,000 users (40 percent times 5,000 kids).

*Three,* you must determine the usage rate per customer, or the average number of days each child will attend day care. Based on industry experience, you conservatively estimate that each child would use the day-care center an average of 90 days per year. Therefore, your market potential, in terms of days used, is 90 days times 2,000 possible users, or 180,000 days.

*Four,* determine your price. Calculate your costs to staff, run, and market your facility. Examine your competitors' prices (including the not-so-obvious competitors such as nannies, babysitters, religious centers). Put a value on the unique and different things you are going to offer. Calculate your breakeven (see previous chapter). You decide your price will be $32 per eight-hour day per kid.

Thus, your total market revenue potential—if you get every kid to come 90 days—is 2,000 kids times 90 days times $32 a day, or $5,760,000.

*Five,* determine a realistic, attainable goal. After research among parents, showing them your plans, you reckon you will be able to get a 10 percent market share, or 200 kids, at 90 days per year. Your 10 percent market share is 18,000 days (200 kids times 90 days). If you sell 18,000 days of day care at $32 per day, your annual revenues will be close to $576,000 (18,000 days times $32 per day.)

You previously calculated your breakeven revenue to be $288,000. If you achieve 50 percent of your annual goal in the first year, which is a 5 percent market share, you will generate revenues of $288,000 and break even. In year two, if you achieve an 8 percent market share, you will have sales of $460,800 and will generate $172,000 after paying for all your costs.

To summarize: To calculate market size you multiply the number of attainable potential customers times the average number of units purchased times the average price per unit purchased. Typically, you do this calculation on an annual basis.

The formula: *# of customers* × *avg. # of units purchased per year* × *avg. $ price per unit* = *$ market potential*.

Market size calculations can be done for any business.

Note to the owner of this exampled day-care center: The market exists. There are customers. Go get them!

## • XLVIII •
## *Getting Start-up Money*

*B*y now you know the size of your market. You know the number of customers to whom you can realistically sell. You know the average number of units each customer will buy. You know the average price per unit. You have determined your total estimated revenue (which you calculated per year or per month, or any time period). You know all your expected costs. The difference between your total revenues and your total costs is the money you will make. You must know these numbers to give confidence to yourself, and to anyone who loans you money that they will get paid back. There are many sources of start-up money:

1. Savings.
2. Loans against your house.
3. Loans against your life insurance.
4. Loans against other assets such as equipment.
5. Loans, gifts, or investments from friends or family.
6. Credit cards.
7. Bank loans.
8. Equity investments (for example, from venture capitalists or angel investors).
9. Selling stock in your company.
10. Severance pay or cashed-in stock options or retirement funds.
11. Lease assets or inventories you intend to buy.
12. Get credit from a supplier.
13. Prebill and collect from customers.
14. Barter (for example, trading legal fees for advertising or vice-versa).
15. Pick up soda cans from the side of the road and collect the deposit money.

There are numerous sources of start-up money, and all have a price. Lenders or investors rent you money, and until you pay it all back, you are charged a monthly rent. (The monthly "rent" is interest on the loan.) Factor into your costs the amount of the money rent (based on interest rates) you must pay. Be sure you can pay the rent.

A business that has good customers now or in its forseeable future can get money today.

# · XLIX ·
## *The Big Money*

*T*here are basically two types of small businesses:
(1) companies that are managed primarily to
provide the owner income to live a certain lifestyle;
and (2) companies that are managed primarily to be
sold. There is often a melding of these two models,
where the lifestyle company possibly has some sale value,
and the company for sale model provides lifestyle income.

Lifestyle companies are often quite small (one to
ten employees); or provide a service, not a product;
or are nonmanufacturing; or some combination. These
companies do not build equity valuable enough for

another entity to buy. These companies provide income to the owners to fund their lifestyle. For example, a Park Avenue psychiatrist's medical practice may generate significant lifestyle revenues and income, but as a saleable business is worth nothing, or relatively little (medical books and a couch?) after the psychiatrist retires.

Companies primarily managed to be sold typically have over fifty employees; or sell a product, not a service; or build some kind of equity that has lasting value and can be sold. For example, the lasting value can be tangible assets, or a strong market share position, good brand names, good location, continuing revenues, product patents. These valuable assets will exist after the business owner sells.

Of the 25 million or so small businesses in the United States, some 20 million are managed primarily as lifestyle businesses. Over 1,000,000 of these businesses provide the owners with annual income upward from $500,000. This is BIG money!

The other 5,000,000 small businesses are managed to be sold . . . someday. The intention to keep a business as a lifestyle company, to keep it privately owned, to keep it in the family, is legitimate. However, almost always, over 98 percent of all non-lifestyle companies are ultimately sold. They are sold to another company, sold to the public, or sold to employees. A mere handful of successful companies are put into a trust, where they are then managed to produce income to fund the trust's purposes. These companies are no longer owned by the owner's family and often are ultimately sold out of the trust.

There are all kinds of ways buyers and sellers put a value, or price, on the worth of a small business. Business sellers set purchase prices based on a multiple of revenue streams (say, one dollar purchase price for every dollar in sales); or on the present value of the company's net worth in five years; or on the intangible value of a brand name; or the value of client lists; or the value of plant, equipment, land; or the untapped potential for growth in sales and profits; or on a multiple of true profit (say, a price that is five times net profit).

For example, if a metal parts manufacturing business has sales of $7,000,000 and profits of $400,000, the sale price could be based on any combination of valuations. There are oodles of factors buyers consider, but for simplicity's sake, in this example, the buyer believes the $7,000,000 in sales will grow about 3 percent a year, and believes there is a $5,000,000 revenue opportunity to sell the metal parts in a totally new market. The buyer calculates that in three years your business will have revenues of $11,000,000 and profits of $600,000. The buyer looks at your products, your markets, your future, and offers to buy your company for $6,000,000 in cash plus absorption of your debt.

You jump on it. That's BIG money!

# Epilogue

You are always your own best investment. So it is never too late to start your own business. Ray Kroc started McDonald's in his fifties. Colonel Sanders started Kentucky Fried Chicken in his sixties. You are never too young to start a business. Michael Dell started Dell Computer while in college. You don't need an MBA to start your own business. Millions of entrepreneurs never graduated from college. Bill Gates dropped out of college to start Microsoft. You don't need to be a man to start a business. Forty-eight percent of all new businesses are started by women.

You don't need a lot of things to start a business . . . but you must have one thing. You must have a customer. Go get that customer.

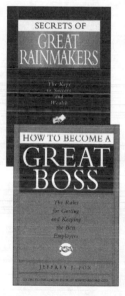

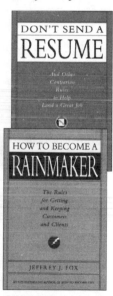